DR. J'S GMAT CRITICAL REASONING

Smart Guide

DR. JYUTHICA. K. LAGHATE

Dedication

I dedicate this solemnly to my parents Late. Mrs. Anuja Pendharkar and Late. Mr. Alhad Pendharkar whose blessings and teachings have been instrumental in motivating me to choose English teaching as my career path and follow my childhood dream. I also want to thank my Almighty for his grace and protection. Last but not the least, a special thanks to my beloved husband for always boosting me to excel and tread on paths unfounded.

Contents

Preface

GMAT Critical Reasoning-Strategies and Solved Questions, is one of its kind fully solved guides about critical reasoning in the Graduate Management Aptitude Test (GMAT). Critical Reasoning is one of the key components of the test with maximum number of questions asked on critical reasoning or logic based reading comprehension. Since the inception of the test, this section has been considered challenging by most candidates, since it requires deeper evaluation of how the different answer options are exactly in line or counter to the conclusion or the claim in the arguments.

On the other side, since, this is based on analytical ability and precise understanding,it is one section ,where full scores can be achieved with a dedicated and deft preparation.This guide exactly focusses on how one can score 100% in this section utilising seemingly simple yet quickest and most effective strategies and tricks.

The book includes numerous question types that are both commonly and rarely asked in the examination. Please note,all the examples have been solved in the most simplest and understandable manner for all candidates who may be having different aptitudes or at variable stages of preparation.

This book is an endeavour to fully support all students in enabling a superlative score in critical reasoning which can help them to score much better in the overall verbal section. All the strategies and tricks have been time tested for more than a decade in my classroom.

Kindly utilise this book as an opportunity to achieve your dream score in GMAT ,which is a brain stimulating and challenging exam ,but it is certainly not an impossible feat and this endeavour can take you one step closer to your ambition.

Best Wishes,

Dr.J

Director, Dr.J's Knowledge Café

Email:jyuths@gmail.com

Chapter 1

Introduction

Critical reasoning contributes to about 40% weightage in the Graduate Management Aptitude test. Out of total 36 questions asked in a 65 minutes verbal section, 14 questions are devoted to **Critical Reasoning**. Needless to say, it is one of the most important sections in the test and requires careful planning, strategising, analysis and interpretation 'to the T'.

What does Critical Reasoning mean in GMAT?

Critical reasoning is a vital skill required for entry level as well as higher end managers and leaders. It is like a set of mandatory competencies required to take balanced, productive and efficacious decisions. Hence, it was introduced in the Graduate Management Aptitude Test ,since a candidate with deft logical reasoning may mean a really deserving candidate to study these incredibly brain stimulating higher education courses such as MBA or Masters in Management and then utilise his/her critical ability in real professional settings.

Critical reasoning or logic based reasoning is therefore a crucial component of the test since its inception. Your next question might be extremely valid..! Critical reasoning is so vast and open ended in terms of its contexts.

So, how is it in this exam and what kind of questions would be posed?

The kind of contexts and areas from which critical reasoning arguments are derived are multi-dimensional from economics to management, films to pharmaceutical industry, food to politics. The spheres are wide but the arguments can be completely decoded and deciphered with structured, wise and creative solving approach. The next relevant question, what are the types of critical reasoning questions asked in the verbal section? Thoroughly going through an array of resources, it is pertinently seen that the kind of questions asked in critical reasoning follow a certain distinct pattern and the commonly asked questions are stated as follows:

1. What is the underlying assumption in the argument?

2. What is the main conclusion in the argument?

3. If the main conclusion is right, what is the second conclusion/or what else must also be true?

4. What if true, weakens the conclusion or argument? or Everything strengthens the argument except…

5. What if true, strengthens the conclusion or argument or resolves a discrepancy or contradiction in the argument?

6. Bold face reasoning

7. Similar reasoning

8. Inference

GOLDEN RULES OF CRITICAL REASONING

1. **Read the question like a hawk spotting its prey.**

   Precise yet detailed and multi-dimensional reading is the key. Breaking the question in terms of what the author has really asked is the key. Different paraphrases of the same question need to be understood.

   E.g; What if true weakens the conclusion is same as everything strengthens the argument except.

   In short, be a 'Hint Hunter'. The clue lies in the question itself.

2. The next step is identifying exactly the main argument, conclusion and facts and premise/assumptions on which the conclusion or argument is based.

   For the sake of simplicity, think of it as the "ACF Factor."

ACF Factor of Critical Reasoning

Assumption

Assumption is the imaginary notion or idea upon which the conclusion is based.

Conclusion

It is the main crux or the final deducing from the argument based on assumption, facts, contexts and trends.

Facts/Premise

This is what is mentioned in the argument as a true finding, data or a matter of fact.

Let us try and understand these fundamental terms better with an actual critical reasoning sample.

Recently an unusually high number of dolphins have been found dead of infectious diseases, and most of these had abnormally high tissue concentrations of certain compounds that, even in low concentrations, reduce dolphins' resistance to infection. The only source of these compounds in the dolphins' environment is boat paint. Therefore, since dolphins rid their bodies of the compounds rapidly once exposure ceases, their mortality rate should decline rapidly if such boat paints are banned.

Which of the following, if true, most strengthens the argument?

Assumption

Only source of these toxic compounds in dolphins' environment is boat paint.

Fact

Recently an unusually high number of dolphins have been found dead of infectious diseases and most of these had abnormally high tissue concentrations of certain compounds that, even in low concentrations, reduce dolphins' resistance to infection.

Conclusion

Based on the assumption and fact, since dolphins rid their bodies of the compounds rapidly once exposure ceases, their mortality rate should decline rapidly if such boat paints are banned.

The question is which option strengthens the main argument?

Hint

Dolphins get rid of these compounds from their body once exposure to them stops and therefore their mortality rate will be reduced once these boat paints are banned.

So, the key is not only banning the boat paints but also the ability of the dolphins to get rid of the toxic compounds after exposure is stopped.

Let us carefully evaluate every option and choose the best answer.

A. The levels of the compounds typically used in boat paints today are lower than they were in boat paints manufactured a decade ago- This is irrelevant to the main conclusion which talks about dolphin's ability to get rid of these compounds from their body.

B. In high concentrations, the compounds are toxic to many types of marine animals- This is a casual generalisation, in the argument dolphins are the point of focus.

C. The compounds break down into harmless substances after a few months of exposure to water or air- This completely nullifies the vital role played by dolphin's body in throwing out the toxic compounds.

D. High tissue levels of the compounds have recently been found in some marine animals, but there is no record of any of those animals dying in unusually large numbers recently-This option perfectly talks about how despite having high levels of compounds found in animals but no record of them dying in high numbers suggesting they were able to get rid of the toxic compounds. Hence, this is the answer.

E. The compounds do not leach out of the boat paint if the paint is applied exactly in accordance with the manufacturer's directions-This completely negates the harmful effect of the boat paint and is thus eliminated.

Chapter 2

Conclusion Based Critical Reasoning

Let us go through these simplest and quickest techniques to master critical reasoning questions by having a detailed insight on all types of critical reasoning questions asked in GMAT.

Solved Problem Set: Based on Conclusion in the Argument as well as if one conclusion is true, what is also true?

1. The greater the division of labour in an economy, the greater the need for coordination. This is because increased division of labour entails a larger number of specialised producers, which results in a greater burden on managers and, potentially, in a greater number of disruptions of supply and production.

   There is always more division of labor in market economies than in planned economies.

   If all of the statements above are true, then which of the following must also be true?

A. Disruptions' of supply and production are more frequent in planned economies than in market economies.

B. There are more specialised producers in planned economies than in market economies.

C. The need for coordination in market economies is greater than in planned economies.

D. A manager's task is easier in a market economy than in a planned economy.

E. Division of labor functions more effectively in market economies than in planned economies.

This question is a case of two conclusions which means, if all the statements given are true, what else must also be true or having the same analogy.

As solved before, the first step in critical reasoning is identifying the main assumptions, facts and conclusion of the argument or what we will call as "ACF Factor" of Critical Reasoning.

There are multiple benefits of identifying the "ACF Factor" such as understanding the overall background of the argument, what precisely the author has based his conclusion/s on and what are the stated and implied (hidden) assumptions that are absolutely pivotal to arrive at the correct answer.

Conclusion

1. Greater division of labour requires greater need for co-ordination.

2. More division of labour is present in market economies than planned economies.

Assumption

Greater need for co-ordination is based on the assumption that increased division of labour entails a larger number of specialised producers, which results in a greater burden on managers and, potentially, in a greater number of disruptions of supply and production.

Hint

Now based on this scenario, we can arrive at a certain inference that since greater division of labour is present in market economy, there is greater need of co-ordination in market economy.

Now, let's see what the answer options are and which fits the best for the scenario.

Focus on Options and Carefully Evaluate and Eliminate the Ones that are Irrelevant or Contradictory to the Facts.

A. Disruptions' of supply and production are more frequent in planned economies than in market economies- The passage says otherwise like disruptions are more in market economies so we eliminate this option.

B. There are more specialised producers in planned economies than in market economies- According to the passage more specialised producers are required where there is more division of labour, that is in market economies, so this option is also ruled out.

C. The need for coordination in market economies is greater than in planned economies. This option is in line with the conclusion, i.e; since division of labour is more in market economies, more co-ordination is needed and therefore is the best possible answer

D. A manager's task is easier in a market economy than in a planned economy- This is against the premise of the passage and thus eliminated.

E. Division of labor functions more effectively in market economies than in planned economies -

This is already mentioned in the passage as a given and we need to find another point of similar comparison and hence crossed out.

Chapter 3

What if true weakens the claim or the conclusion of the argument?

This is one of the most vital and frequently asked critical reasoning question type and therefore must not be ignored. Daily practice of atleast 5 questions based on this category will be immensely useful to understand the wide range of conclusion weakening scenarios that are thrown at you in the exam.

Solved Problem Set:

1. A program instituted in a particular state allows parents to prepay their children's future college tuition at current rates. The program then pays the tuition annually for the child at any of the state's public colleges in which the child enrolls. Parents should participate in the program as a means of decreasing the cost for their children's college education.

   Which of the following, if true, is the most appropriate reason for parents NOT to participate in the program?

   A. The parents are unsure about which public college in the state the child will attend.

B. The amount of money accumulated by putting the prepayment funds in an interest-bearing account today will be greater than the total cost of tuition for any of the public colleges when the child enrolls.

C. The annual cost of tuition at the state's public colleges is expected to increase at a faster rate than the annual increase in the cost of living.

D. Some of the state's public colleges are contemplating large increases in tuition next year.

E. The prepayment plan would not cover the cost of room and board at any of the state's public colleges.

Conclusion

Participating in the program to prepay for children's future will be a means of decreasing the cost of their children's college education.

Assumption

The program will allow parents to prepay and then pay the tuition annually to facilitate the child enrollment in any public college in the state.

Question

Which of the following, if true, is the most appropriate reason for parents NOT to participate in the program?

Solution – B

A. The parents are unsure about which public college in the state the child will attend – This partially addresses the issue but does not speak about cost decrease or effectiveness.

B. The amount of money accumulated by putting the prepayment funds in an interest-bearing account today will be greater than the total cost of tuition for any of the public colleges when the child enrolls- This option definitely provides a better financial cost reduction or infact accumulation to the parents, which they can consider as a valid point to not participate and will pay later on their own instead of enrolling in prepayment and losing on this interest amount. Therefore, Option B is the answer.

C. The annual cost of tuition at the state's public colleges is expected to increase at a faster rate than the annual increase in the cost of living- This seems to be a casual prediction which may not be the reality.

D. Some of the state's public colleges are contemplating large increases in tuition next year- Again, it might just be a consideration and not a fixed outcome.

E. The prepayment plan would not cover the cost of room and board at any of the state's public colleges- This also is not mentioned in the argument and seems to be a casual generalisation.

2. Insurance Company X is considering issuing a new policy to cover services required by elderly

people who suffer from diseases that afflict the elderly. Premiums for the policy must be low enough to attract customers. Therefore, Company X is concerned that the income from the policies would not be sufficient to pay for the claims that would be made.

Which of the following strategies would be most likely to minimize Company X's losses on the policies?

A. Attracting middle-aged customers unlikely to submit claims for benefits for many years.

B. Insuring only those individuals who did not suffer any serious diseases as children

C. Including a greater number of services in the policy than are included in other policies of lower cost

D. Insuring only those individuals who were rejected by other companies for similar policies

E. Insuring only those individuals who are wealthy enough to pay for the medical services

Conclusion

Since premiums are low, therefore, Company X is concerned that the income from the policies would not be sufficient to pay for the claims that would be made.

Assumption

Premiums must be low to attract customers.

Question

The question is framed in a different way. But, it actually focusses on what if true weakens the claim and losses will likely be minimised.

Solution – A

A. Attracting middle-aged customers unlikely to submit claims for benefits for many years- This can certainly minimise losses of the company since the customers unlikely to submit claims would mean less load on the insurance company and therefore is the answer.

B. Insuring only those individuals who did not suffer any serious diseases as children – This does not guarantee that these individuals won't fall sick when they are older and therefore can be eliminated.

C. Including a greater number of services in the policy than are included in other policies of lower cost – This will result in higher losses due to lower cost and more services provided by the company.

D. Insuring only those individuals who were rejected by other companies for similar policies – This also strengthens the concern of the author that losses will be incurred because these individuals will be likely to claim for benefit to this agency since they are rejected by the rest.

E. Insuring only those individuals who are wealthy enough to pay for the medical services- Insuring richer people will still not bridge the gap between lower premiums and higher cost for the insurance agency.

3. A common defense of sport hunting is that it serves 'a vital wildlife-management function, without which countless animals would succumb to starvation and disease. This defense leads to the overly hasty conclusion that sport hunting produces a healthier population of animals.

Which of the following, if true, best supports the author's claim that sport hunting does not necessarily produce a healthier population of animals?

A. For many economically depressed families, hunting helps keep food on the table.

B. Wildlife species encroach on fann crops when other food supplies become scarce.

C. Overpopulation of a species causes both strong and weak animals to suffer.

D. Sport hunters tend to pursue the biggest and healthiest animals in a population.

E. Many people have strong moral objections to killing a creature for any reason other than self-defense.

Conclusion

It is stated hasty by the author that sport hunting produces a healthier population of animals.

Assumption

A common defense of sport hunting is that it serves 'a vital wildlife-management function, without which countless animals would succumb to starvation and disease. So, in simple words, sport hunting is said to save animals from starvation and disease.

Question

The question demands to choose an option that supports the opposite claim that hunting does not necessarily produce healthier animals.

Solution – D

A. For many economically depressed families, hunting helps keep food on the table – This goes off the point about healthier animals and therefore eliminated.

B. Wildlife species encroach on fann crops when other food supplies become scarce- Again, an irrelevant point about wildlife encroaching on other species.

C. Overpopulation of a species causes both strong and weak animals to suffer- The whole argument is about healthier animals and not overpopulation.

D. Sport hunters tend to pursue the biggest and healthiest animals in a population- This weakens the claim that sport hunting produces healthier animals whereas hunting actually preys upon the biggest and healthiest animals in a population and therefore is the best possible answer.

E. Many people have strong moral objections to killing a creature for any reason other than self-defense- This is again off the main point.

4. A worldwide ban on the production of certain ozone-destroying chemicals would provide only an illusion of protection. Quantities of such chemicals, already produced, exist as coolants in millions of refrigerators. When they reach the ozone layer in the atmosphere, their action cannot be halted. So, there is no way to prevent these chemicals from damaging the ozone layer further.

Which of the following, if true, most seriously weakens the argument above?

A. It is impossible to measure with accuracy the quantity of ozone-destroying chemicals that exist as coolants in refrigerators.

B. In modern societies, refrigeration of food is necessary to prevent health and potentially life-threatening conditions.

C. Replacement chemicals that will not destroy ozone have not yet been developed and would be more expensive than the chemicals now used as coolants in refrigerators.

D. Even if people should give up the use of refrigeration, the coolants already in existing refrigerators are a threat to atmospheric ozone.

E. The coolants in refrigerators can be fully recovered at the end of the useful life of the refrigerators and reused.

Conclusion – A

Worldwide ban on the production of certain ozone-destroying chemicals would provide only an illusion of protection. There is no way to prevent these chemicals from damaging the ozone layer further.

Assumption

Quantities of such chemicals, already produced, exist as coolants in millions of refrigerators. When they reach the ozone layer in the atmosphere, their action cannot be halted.

Solution – E

A. It is impossible to measure with accuracy the quantity of ozone-destroying chemicals that exist as coolants in refrigerators- This is off the point because measuring accurately the quantity of ozone destroying chemicals has no correlation to its action.

B. In modern societies, refrigeration of food is necessary to prevent health and potentially life-threatening conditions-Again a vast generalisation that does not throw light on the main argument.

C. Replacement chemicals that will not destroy ozone have not yet been developed and would be more expensive than the chemicals now used as coolants in refrigerators- This point too talks about a different issue of cost and development of replacement chemicals.

D. Even if people should give up the use of refrigeration, the coolants already in existing refrigerators are a threat to atmospheric ozone- This point strengthens the main conclusion and we are looking for an answer that will weaken the conclusion.

E. The coolants in refrigerators can be fully recovered at the end of the useful life of the refrigerators and reused- This option seriously weakens the conclusion that the coolants can be reused and therefore will not be released in the atmosphere and not prove a threat.

5. Although the human population around the forestland in Middlesex County has increased, the amount of forestland has not been reduced. Therefore, the decrease in the county's songbird population cannot be attributed to the growth 'in the county's human population.

Which of the following, if true, most seriously weakens the conclusion above?

A. As the human population of Middlesex County has grown, there has been an increase in the number of shopping malls built.

B. The presence of more garbage cans resulting from the increase in the county's human population ensures the survival of more raccoons, which prey on songbird eggs whenever available.

C. There has recently been a decrease in the amount of rain-forest land in Central and South America, where songbirds spend the winter months.

D. Although several species of songbirds are disappearing from Middlesex County, these species are far from being endangered.

E. The disappearance of songbirds, which eat insects, often results in increased destruction of trees by insects.

Conclusion

The decrease in the county's songbird population cannot be attributed to the growth 'in the county's human population.

Assumption

Although the human population around the forestland in Middlesex County has increased, the amount of forestland has not been reduced.

Question

Which of the following, if true, most seriously weakens the conclusion above?

Solution – B

Now, we need to look for an option that weakens the conclusion and highlights the fact that the songbird

population has been reduced because of human population.

A. As the human population of Middlesex County has grown, there has been an increase in the number of shopping malls built- This does not include the basic premise of songbird reduction.

B. The presence of more garbage cans resulting from the increase in the county's human population ensures the survival of more raccoons, which prey on songbird eggs whenever available- This option mentions a clear cut human mention of survival of raccoons who eat songbird eggs and therefore, the songbird population has reduced. This is the best possible answer.

C. There has recently been a decrease in the amount of rain-forest land in Central and South America, where songbirds spend the winter months- This may mean songbirds would migrate somewhere else and their population might increase.

D. Although several species of songbirds are disappearing from Middlesex County, these species are far from being endangered- This states that species are not reducing so much to be extinct and clearly is opposite of the main argument.

E. The disappearance of songbirds, which eat insects, often results in increased destruction of trees by insects- This is completely off the point.

Chapter 4

What is the underlying or the basic assumption in the argument?

Understanding the basic assumption is the pivot of critical reasoning success. All arguments posed in the exam are based on certain explicit and certain implied assumptions. The kind of assumptions asked here are the implied or the implicit ones.

1. According to one psychological theory, in order to be happy, one must have an 'intimate relationship with another person. Yet the world's greatest composers spent most of their time in solitude and had no intimate relationships. So the psychological theory must be wrong.

The conclusion above assumes that

A. The world's greatest composers chose to avoid intimate relationships

B. People who have intimate relationships spend little time in solitude

C. Solitude is necessary for the composition of great music

D. Less well known composers had intimate relationships

E. The world's greatest composers were happy

Conclusion

The psychological theory must be wrong because the world's greatest composers spent most of their time in solitude and had no intimate relationships.

Assumptions

According to one psychological theory, in order to be happy, one must have an 'intimate relationship with another person.

The use of 'Yet' here is vital because it gives us a clue that the greatest composers were happy despite being alone and not in intimate relationships.

Solution – E

A. the world's greatest composers chose to avoid intimate relationships- This is not the main assumption.

B. people who have intimate relationships spend little time in solitude- This is an extreme generalization, we can't really conclude that all people who have intimate relationships spend little time in solitude.

C. solitude is necessary for the composition of great music- This also cannot be concluded from this argument.

D. less well known composers had intimate relationships- Again a casual generalisation.

E. the world's greatest composers were happy- The use of 'Yet' in the conclusion is vital because it gives us a clue that the greatest composers were happy despite being alone and not in intimate relationships and therefore the theory that in order to be happy one needs to be in intimate relationships seems to be wrong and this is the **right answer**.

2. Riothamus, a fifth-century king of the Britons, was betrayed by an associate, fought bravely against the Goths but was defeated, and disappeared mysteriously.Riothamus' activities, and only those of Riothamus, match almost exactly those attributed to King Arthur. Therefore, Riothamus must be the historical model for the legendary King Arthur.

The argument above requires at least one additional premise. Which of the following could be such a required premise?

A. Modern historians have documented the activities of Riothamus better than those of any other fifth-century king.

B. The stories told about King Arthur are not strictly fictitious but are based on a historical person and historical events.

C. Riothamus' associates were the authors of the original legends about King Arthur.

D. Legends about the fifth century usually embellish and romanticize the actual conditions of the lives of fifth-century nobility.

E.   Posterity usually remembers legends better than it remembers the actual historical events on which they are based.

Conclusion

Therefore, Riothamus must be the historical model for the legendary King Arthur.

Assumption

Riothamus' activities, and only those of Riothamus, match almost exactly those attributed to King Arthur.

Question

What is one additional premise or assumption that is also required for this argument?

Solution – B

A.   Modern historians have documented the activities of Riothamus better than those of any other fifth-century king. – This can't be concluded on the basis of this argument.

B.   The stories told about King Arthur are not strictly fictitious but are based on a historical person and historical events- We can perfectly come to the conclusion that Riothamus's activities match to those of King Arthur only if the stories about King Arthur are real and based on the actual person and events. Therefore,this option rightly is the second premise required for the argument to hold true.

C. Riothamus' associates were the authors of the original legends about King Arthur- That does not prove the point that Riothamus's activities match that of Arthur.

D. Legends about the fifth century usually embellish and romanticize the actual conditions of the lives of fifth-century nobility- A casual generalisation.

E. Posterity usually remembers legends better than it remembers the actual historical events on which they are based- An extremely biased conclusion that only legends are remembered and not historical events.

3. Unlike other retail outlets, where items are purchased in any number of units the customer wants, in super-markets items are grouped in bulk packages. This bulk buying offers savings to the customer. The option to buy at wholesale prices by buying in bulk makes super-markets a practical choice for budget-conscious consumers.

Which of the following is an assumption necessary to the author's argument?

A. Super-markets often have greater buying power and lower overhead costs, so they can offer a greater variety of products than regular retail outlets.

B. Super-markets are often more conveniently located and have better parking facilities.

C. The emergence of super-markets has caused many small retail stores to close down and thus eliminate competition.

D. It is economically wise to buy single items since bulk packages seldom offer significant savings.

E. The financial savings from purchasing bulk packages may outweigh the inconvenience of being unable to purchase in any number of units that suits the customers' need.

Conclusion

The option to buy at wholesale prices by buying in bulk makes super-markets a practical choice for budget-conscious consumers.

Assumption

This bulk buying in super markets offers savings to the customer.

Question

Assumption in the argument?

Solution – E

A. Super-markets often have greater buying power and lower overhead costs, so they can offer a greater variety of products than regular retail outlets- This is an irrelevant point since the main argument is about supermarkets being a practical choice.

B. Super-markets are often more conveniently located and have better parking facilities-

Again ,this does not completely explain why supermarkets are best for budget conscious customers.

C. The emergence of super-markets has caused many small retail stores to close down and thus eliminate competition- Completely off the point.

D. It is economically wise to buy single items since bulk packages seldom offer significant savings- Extreme conclusion which might be actually wrong in many cases.

E. The financial savings from purchasing bulk packages may outweigh the inconvenience of being unable to purchase in any number of units that suits the customers' need- This option throws light on the main assumption about the fact that buying in bulk in supermarkets actually results in better savings and outweighs the inconveniences it causes to not get a chance to buy only what is needed and therefore the **right answer**.

4. The federal government expects hospitals to perform 10,000 organ transplants next year. But it is doubtful that this many donor organs will be available, since the number of fatalities resulting from car and motorcycle accidents have been dropping steadily over the past decade.

The argument above makes which of the following assumptions?

A. A significant number of the organs used in transplants come from people who die in car and motorcycle accidents.

B. The number of car and motorcycle accidents will increase significantly during the next year.

C. No more than 10,000 people will be in need of organ transplants during the next year.

D. In the past the federal government's estimates of the number of organ transplants needed during a given year have been very unreliable.

E. For any given fatality resulting from a car or motorcycle accident, there is a hospital in the vicinity in need' of an organ for a transplant.

Conclusion

It is doubtful that this many donor organs will be available.

Premise

Since the number of fatalities resulting from car and motorcycle accidents have been dropping steadily over the past decade.

Solution – A

A. A significant number of the organs used in transplants come from people who die in car and motorcycle accidents- This is the most logical assumption and the answer because federal government has said that they require 10,000 transplants but it is doubtful to achieve since car and motorcycle accidents have reduced. This means they believe that the majority of organs will be obtained from these accident dead bodies.

B. The number of car and motorcycle accidents will increase significantly during the next year- This is a future prediction which does not help the current scenario.

C. No more than 10,000 people will be in need of organ transplants during the next year- Again a future entity that is not relevant.

D. In the past the federal government's estimates of the number of organ transplants needed during a given year have been very unreliable- This is a trap because although past estimates might be unreliable, that doesn't mean the current predictions are unreliable.

E. For any given fatality resulting from a car or motorcycle accident, there is a hospital in the vicinity in need' of an organ for a transplant- This seems to be an extreme generalisation which might be untrue.

5. One of the world's most celebrated paintings, The Man with the Golden Helmet, long attributed to Rembrandt, is not a Rembrandt after all. So say several art experts, who base their conclusion on an analysis of stylistic features, especially details both of shading and of brushwork. In

order to ascertain who really painted the well-known masterpiece, the experts have begun a series of sophisticated new tests, including one that involves the activation of neutrons. These tests yield patterns for any painters that are as distinctive as a good set of fingerprints.

Which of the following is an assumption on which the conclusion of the art experts depends?

A. The Man with the Golden Helmet was riot painted during Rembrandt's lifetime.

B. If even The Man with the Golden Helmet is of questionable attribution, then any supposedly authentic Rembrandt has now become suspect.

C. The painting known as The Man with the Golden Helmet is a copy of a Rembrandt original.

D. The original ascription of The Man with the Golden Helmet to Rembrandt was a deliberate fraud.

E. There are significant consistencies among authentic Rembrandts in certain matters of style.

Conclusion

According to the art experts, one of the world's most celebrated paintings, The Man with the Golden Helmet, long attributed to Rembrandt, is not a Rembrandt after all. They have based their conclusion on an analysis of stylistic features, especially details both of shading and of brushwork.

Premise

In order to ascertain who really painted the well-known masterpiece, the experts began a series of sophisticated new tests, including one that involves the activation of neutrons. These tests yield patterns for any painters that are as distinctive as a good set of fingerprints.

Solution – E

A. The Man with the Golden Helmet was riot painted during Rembrandt's lifetime- The information about Man with a Golden Helmet is not the assumption and therefore rejected.

B. If even The Man with the Golden Helmet is of questionable attribution, then any supposedly authentic Rembrandt has now become suspect- This also can't be the assumption behind the validity of the tests to check whether Rembrandt was the same author based on his stylistic patterns.

C. The painting known as The Man with the Golden Helmet is a copy of a Rembrandt original- Again this is off the point.

D. The original ascription of The Man with the Golden Helmet to Rembrandt was a deliberate fraud- This is another point of deviation.

E. There are significant consistencies among authentic Rembrandts in certain matters of style- The fact that the stylistic patterns are tested to attribute the work to Rembrandt is based on the assumption that there might be some similarities or consistencies amongst various works of Rembrandt and hence would be easy to identify him as the painter. Thus, this is the answer.

Chapter 5

What if true strengthens the argument? OR What if true solves the apparent contradiction in the argument?

1. The average life expectancy for the United States population as a whole is 73.9 years, but children born in Hawaii will live an average of 77 years, and those born in Louisiana, 71.7 years. If a newlywed couple from Louisiana were to begin their family in Hawaii, therefore, their children would be expected to live longer than would be the case if the family remained in Louisiana.

Which of the following statements, if true, would most significantly strengthen the conclusion drawn in the passage?

   A. As population density increases in Hawaii, life expectancy figures for that state are likely to be revised downward.

   B. Environmental factors tending to favor longevity are abundant in Hawaii and less numerous in Louisiana.

C. Twenty-five percent of all Louisianans who move to Hawaii live longer than 77 years.

D. Over the last decade, average life expectancy has risen at a higher rate for Louisianans than for Hawaiians.

E. Studies show that the average life expectancy for Hawaiians who move permanently to Louisiana is roughly equal to that of Hawaiians who remain in Hawaii.

Conclusion

If a newlywed couple from Louisiana were to begin their family in Hawaii, therefore, their children would be expected to live longer than would be the case if the family remained in Louisiana.

Assumption

Life expectancy and living conditions are better in Hawaii than Louisiana.

Solution – B

A. As population density increases in Hawaii, life expectancy figures for that state are likely to be revised downward- This weakens the main conclusion.

B. Environmental factors tending to favor longevity are abundant in Hawaii and less numerous in Louisiana- This provides the additional support for the argument conclusion to be true and therefore is the right answer since environmental factors favouring longevity in Hawaii could lead to a higher life expectancy.

C. Twenty-five percent of all Louisianans who move to Hawaii live longer than 77 years- This is slightly off the point that Hawaii is better than Louisiana.

D. Over the last decade, average life expectancy has risen at a higher rate for Louisianans than for Hawaiians- This is counter to the main conclusion since it says Louisiana has better life expectancy.

E. Studies show that the average life expectancy for Hawaiians who move permanently to Louisiana is roughly equal to that of Hawaiians who remain in Hawaii- Again, this weakens the main point.

2. When an osprey (a fish-eating hawk) returns from fishing to its nesting area with a fish like an alewife, a pollack, or a smelt, other ospreys will retrace its flight path in hopes of good fishing. There is seldom such a response if the first bird brings back a winter flounder. Yet ospreys feed on winter flounder just as readily as on any other fish.

Which of the following, if true, contributes most to an explanation of the fishing behavior of ospreys as it is described above?

A. Ospreys are seldom able to catch alewives, pollack, or smelt.

B. Alewives, pollack, and smelt move in schools, but winter flounder do not.

C. Winter flounder prefer shallower waters than do alewives, pollack, or smelt.

D. Winter flounder and pollack exhibit protective coloration, but alewives and smelt do not.

E. Ospreys that live in nesting areas are especially successful fishers.

Conclusion

Yet ospreys feed on winter flounder just as readily as on any other fish.

Assumption

When an osprey (a fish-eating hawk) returns from fishing to its nesting area with a fish like an alewife, a pollack, or smelt, other ospreys will retrace its flight path in hopes of good fishing. There is seldom such a response if the first bird brings back a winter flounder.

A. Ospreys are seldom able to catch alewives, pollack, or smelt- This is against the data in the argument.

B. Alewives, pollack, and smelt move in schools, but winter flounder do not- This does not provide explanation of fishing behaviour of ospreys.

C. Winter flounder prefer shallower waters than do alewives, pollack, or smelt- This is an intricate point about winter flounder which is not the main focus of the argument.

D. Winter flounder and pollack exhibit protective coloration, but alewives and smelt do not-An allied point which is not the part of the main argument.

E. Ospreys that live in nesting areas are especially successful fishers- This provides the most logical explanation of the fishing behaviour of ospreys, that they are successful fishers, preying on lot of fish.

3. In October 1987 the United States stock market suffered a major drop in prices. During the weeks after the drop, the volume of stocks traded also dropped sharply to well below what had been the weekly average of the preceding year. However, the volume for the entire year was not appreciably sdifferent from the preceding year's volume.

Which of the following, if true, resolves the apparent contradiction presented in the passage above?

A. Foreign investors usually buy United States stocks only when prices are low.

B. The number of stock buyers in 1987 remained about the same as it had been the preceding year.

C. For some portion of 1987, the volume of stocks traded was higher than the average for that year.

D. The greater the volume of stocks traded in a given year, the lower the average price per share on the United States stock market for that year.

    E. The volume of stocks traded rises and falls in predictable cycles.

Conclusion

In 1987, US stock market suffered a major drop in prices and the volume of stocks traded also dropped sharply to well below the weekly average of the preceding year.

Assumption

The volume for the entire year was not appreciably different from the previous year's volume.

Solution – C

    A. Foreign investors usually buy United States stocks only when prices are low- This does not explain the relationship between the volumes of stocks traded in both the years.

    B. The number of stock buyers in 1987 remained about the same as it had been the preceding year- Number of stock buyers remaining constant may not mean the volumes traded are the same.

    C. For some portion of 1987, the volume of stocks traded was higher than the average for that year- Although the volume of the stocks traded was lower weeks after the prices are dropped, in the whole year there was a time where they were traded at higher prices and therefore, it evened out and there was no appreciable difference between 1986 and 1987.Thus,this is the correct answer that solves the apparent contradiction in the argument, that although the volumes had fallen, there was no striking difference between the two years.

D. The greater the volume of stocks traded in a given year, the lower the average price per share on the United States stock market for that year- This is an accessory point,not the main premise.

E. The volume of stocks traded rises and falls in predictable cycles- A casual generalisation that does not solve the contradiction.

Chapter 6

Less Commonly asked Critical Reasoning Categories

1. Author Implication/Implied Reasoning

This is one of the less commonly asked critical reasoning categories and requires the candidate to understand what the author really wants to say when he concludes or assumes.

1. A placebo is a chemically inert substance prescribed more for the mental relief of a patient than for its effect on the patient's physical disorder. It is prescribed in the hope of instilling in the patient a positive attitude toward prospects for his or her recovery. In some cases, the placebo actually produces improvement in the patient's condition. In discussing the use and effect of placebos, a well-known medical researcher recently paid physicians the somewhat offbeat compliment of saying that physicians were the ultimate placebo.

By comparing a physician to a placebo, the researcher sought to imply that

A. Physicians should always maintain and communicate an optimistic attitude toward their patients, regardless of the prognosis.

B. The health of some patients can improve simply from their knowledge that they are under a physician's care.

C. Many patients actually suffer from imagined illnesses that are best treated by placebos.

D. Physicians could prescribe less medication and achieve the same effect.

E. It is difficult to determine what, if any, effect a physician's behavior has on a patient's condition.

Conclusion

In discussing the use and effect of placebos, a well-known medical researcher recently paid physicians the somewhat offbeat compliment of saying that physicians were the ultimate placebo.

Assumption

A placebo is a chemically inert substance prescribed more for the mental relief of a patient than for its effect on the patient's physical disorder. It is prescribed in the hope of instilling in the patient a positive attitude toward prospects for his or her recovery.

Solution – A

A. Physicians should always maintain and communicate an optimistic attitude toward their patients, regardless of the prognosis- When the author says, placebo is prescribed in hope of instilling a positive attitude in a patient towards the outcome of his treatment, some where the author implies, physicians should also maintain and communicate a positive attitude when he conveys that the medical researchers said physicians were the ultimate placebos and is therefore the answer.

B. The health of some patients can improve simply from their knowledge that they are under a physician's care- This is a deviation from the main point about comparison between placebos and physician care.

C. Many patients actually suffer from imagined illnesses that are best treated by placebos- This is off the main point.

D. Physicians could prescribe less medication and achieve the same effect-A casual conclusion without any evidence in the argument.

E. It is difficult to determine what, if any, effect, a physician's behavior has on a patient's condition- Again an unsupported conclusion.

2. Describe a Flaw/Correct a discrepancy in the Argument

In this type of critical reasoning, it is expected of the student to identify the inbuilt flaw in the argument as well as what solution could logically correct the discrepancy or defect in the argument.

1. Private ownership of services traditionally considered to be the responsibility of the

government will typically improve those services. The turnpike system in the United States of the nineteenth century demonstrates the truth of this principle; the system,which had previously been controlled by the government,became a more reliable system when taken over by private organizations.

Which of the following describes a significant flaw in the author's argument above?

    A. The author defends the conclusion by appealing to a person of authority.

    B. The author distorts an opposing view in trying to show its weaknesses.

    C. The author defends what the author perceives as a wrong action by pointing out another perceived wrong action.

    D. The author generalizes from a sample not representative enough to establish the conclusion.

    E. The author attributes two very different meanings to the same word.

In this argument, the author concludes drastically that private ownership of all services traditionally handled by government will improve these services.

This conclusion is extreme and based on data of a single system (Turn pike system) that turned more reliable due to private organisational input.

As clearly seen, this is a generalised assumption not adequately supported with just one example and is not representative of all the tasks of the government and the success of the private organisations in those tasks.

From the answer options, it can be observed that:

Option A is not relevant because the author is not defending the conclusion by appealing.

Option B is wrong since the author is supporting his view with a scenario and not showing its weaknesses.

Option C is out of scope because it is not about perceived wrong action by him or anyone else.

Option D is the most logically acceptable and correct answer since the author does generalise and overestimate success of private organizations from a sample not representative enough to draw the conclusion.

Option E is incorrect since it is certainly not about different meanings of the same word.

3. Inference Type of Questions

You may think what the difference between conclusion and inference? They seem to be similar. Not a sin to think that! But, as far as logic based reading comprehension is concerned, inference is something ,we derive from the assumptions and conclusion already there in the argument.

1. A few people who are bad writers simply cannot improve their writing, whether or not they receive instruction. Still, most bad writers can at least be taught to improve their writing enough so that

they are no longer bad writers. However, no one can become a great writer simply by being taught how to be a better writer, since great writers must have not only skill but also talent.

Which one of the following can be properly inferred from the passage above?

    A. All bad writers can become better writers.

    B. All great writers had to be taught to become better writers.

    C. Some bad writers can never become great writers.

    D. Some bad writers can become great writers.

    E. Some great writers can be taught to be even better writers.

After carefully reading the argument, there can be a couple of conclusions. But, the key is which is most accurate, precise and wholistic one and that will be the answer.

    Let us figure that out.

    1. Some bad writers can never become better or improve despite instruction.

    2. All great writers must have talent along with skill.

Now, let us apply these conclusions and come to an answer.

    A. All bad writers can become better writers-This option states that all bad writers can become a better writer which is an extreme.

B. All great writers had to be taught to become better writers- This is also against the main premise.

C. Some bad writers can never become great writers- This supports the main answer that bad writers can become slightly better but need talent and therefore can't become great writers.

D. Some bad writers can become great writers – This is opposite to the main conclusion.

E. Some great writers can be taught to be even better writers- This is also not supporting the main premise which they need talent and not just skill.

4. Bold Face Reasoning

In bold face reasoning, the first step is to understand the nature of relationship between the two highlighted sentences.

The most common themes are either:

1. The first sentence is a claim, the second an evidence against it.

2. The first is a prediction, the second assumption upon which it is based.

3. Cause and effect relationship.

4. The first is a conclusion and second sentence is the intermediary conclusion.

5. Parallel statements or themes.

Once the nature of relationship is determined, the second step is to identify the word clues that can take you closer towards the answer such as " may result" or "will cause" is a prediction or outcome, "yet", "but", "nevertheless" are counter to the claim.Words like "argue", "counterclaim" suggest opposite ideas and assert indicates a strong claim.

Let us apply these strategies and solve bold face reasoning examples as below:

1. Political analyst: A party that temporarily positions itself in the negligible crack between the American right and left will do little to expand the public debate. What America needs is a permanent third party. **Some claim that America's success stems from the two party system**. These people say that a third party would make the passage of legislation and thus governance impossible. Furthermore, they point to the current sluggish pace of government as proof that the country cannot bear the burden of a third party. **Yet, most European countries have multi-party systems and few complain about any inability to govern there.**

Which of the following best describes the functions of the two sections in boldface in the argument above?

   A. The first is the main point of the argument; the second is a premise that supports that point.

   B. The first opposes the premises of the argument; the second is the claim that the argument supports.

C. The first supports the main position held by opponents of the main point; the second is a premise that argues against that position.

D. The first is the primary claim made by opponents of the main point of the argument; the second is evidence proposed in opposition to the first.

E. The first is a claim made by opponents of the main point of the argument; the second is the claim that the first opposes.

Relationship between the highlighted sentences:

First Sentence-Some claim that America's success stems from the two party system. This claim is counter to the conclusion in the first line which states that America needs a third party for proper governance.

Second Sentence- Yet, most European countries have multi-party systems and few complain about any inability to govern there.

This is against the first sentence suggesting that there is evidence that many European countries have multiple parties and no complaints about inability to govern have been seen.Now, let us apply this analogy to the options and find an answer.

A. The first is the main point of the argument; the second is a premise that supports that point- The main point is about the need for America to have a third party ,thus ,this option is eliminated.

B. The first opposes the premises of the argument; the second is the claim that the argument supports- The second is not the claim but the evidence which opposed claim in the first highlighted sentence and is therefore rejected.

C. The first supports the main position held by opponents of the main point; the second is a premise that argues against that position- The first is the main claim and does not support the main position held by opponents.

D. The first is the primary claim made by opponents of the main point of the argument; the second is evidence proposed in opposition to the first- This option is the most holistic option and the answer.since the first line is a primary claim made by opponents of main point that multi party system is essential. The second line is evidence supporting the main point that multi party systems are successful and therefore counter to the first highlighted line.

E. The first is a claim made by opponents of the main point of the argument; the second is the claim that the first opposes.-The second is not the claim but evidence that the first highlighted line opposes and hence rejected.

2. Scientist: Evolutionary biology has long held that the most attractive males of a species, defined as those with the highest quality physical traits that

have no Darwinian survival value, will draw the most female mates. **The resulting male offspring will inherit that attractiveness and themselves have more children as a result,** thus ensuring widespread dissemination of the grandparents' genes. Recently, however, scientists have found that the sons of "high quality" male flycatchers failed to inherit the father's mating status. **Further, the most attractive males were so busy mating that they neglected their offspring; as a result, the sons of homelier birds, who took better care of their offspring, had more success at propagating the species.**

The two portions in boldface play which of the following roles in the scientist's argument?

A. The first is the conclusion of a theory disputed by the scientist; the second is the scientist's new contention based upon the latest evidence.

B. The first is a premise of a long-held biological theory; the second is an example of how this theory works.

C. The first is an explanation of how a biological theory is thought to work; the second is an example of research results that do not support this theory.

D. The first is an example of a theory that used to be prevalent; the second is the new theory that is now considered predominant by scientists.

E. The first introduces a long-held theory that the scientist is going to disprove; the second is the scientist's new theory to replace the one she disproved.

Relationship between the highlighted sentences:

First Sentence

The resulting male offspring from the most attractive male species will inherit that attractiveness and therefore will have more children as a result.

Second Sentence

Further, the most attractive males were so busy mating that they neglected their offspring; as a result, the sons of homelier birds, who took better care of their offspring, had more success at propagating the species. This is additional finding form the scientist's study who found that the sons of high quality males failed to inherit father's mating status.

So,the relationship here is of a claim arising from primary conclusion that attractive males' male offspring will be attractive and have more children and the evidence against the claim.

Now let us try and find the answer.

The two portions in boldface play which of the following roles in the scientist's argument?

A. The first is the conclusion of a theory disputed by the scientist; the second is the scientist's new contention based upon the latest evidence- The first conclusion is not disputed by the scientist.

B. The first is a premise of a long-held biological theory; the second is an example of how this theory works- The second is not an example of how this theory works but is counter to the theory.

C. The first is an explanation of how a biological theory is thought to work; the second is an example of research results that do not support this theory- The first is a claim based upon how the biological theory will work and second is about research findings that go against the theory and thus ,this is the right answer.

D. The first is an example of a theory that used to be prevalent; the second is the new theory that is now considered predominant by scientists.- The first is not an example of a theory that used to be prevalent.

E. The first introduces a long-held theory that the scientist is going to disprove; the second is the scientist's new theory to replace the one she disproved- The scientist is not going to disprove this long held theory and second is not a theory but a finding.

Chapter 7

Additional Practice Exercises

1. The overall operating costs borne by many small farmers are reduced when the farmers eliminate expensive commercial chemical fertilizers and pesticides in favor of crop rotation and the twice-yearly use of manure as fertilizer. Therefore, large farmers should adopt the same measures. They will then realize even greater total savings than do the small farmers.

The argument-above assumes that

   A. It is more cost-effective for small farmers to eliminate the use of commercial fertilizers and pesticides than it is for large farmers to do so.

   B. A sufficient amount of manure will be available for the fields of large farmers.

   C. Large farmers would not realize similar cost benefits by using treated sewage sludge instead of commercial chemical fertilizers.

   D. Large farmers generally look to small farmers for innovative ways of increasing crop yields or reducing operating costs.

   E. The smaller the farm, the more control the farmer has over operating costs.

2. Some insects are able to feed on the leaves of milkweed, a toxic plant, by first cutting and draining the vein that secretes the toxin. This method of detoxification guarantees that some insects will always be able to eat milkweed, because the plant could never evolve to produce a toxin that is lethal in the trace amounts left after the vein is cut.

The conclusion drawn in the passage above depends on which of the following assumptions?

A. The insects that successfully detoxify milkweed are not able to undergo the evolutionary changes necessary to allow them to detoxify other plants.

B. Unlike milkweed, other kinds of toxic plants would be able to overcome their vulnerabilities to predators through evolutionary changes.

C. The toxin-carrying veins of the milkweed plant can never evolve in such a way that insects cannot cut through.

D. The method of detoxification used by insect predators of milkweed would not successfully detoxify other kinds of toxic plants.

E. There are insects that use means other than draining the toxin in order to feed on toxic plants.

3. Researchers studying sets of identical twins who were raised apart in dissimilar environments found that in each case the twins were similar in

character,medical history, and life experiences. The researchers saw these results as confirmation of the hypothesis that heredity is more important than environment in determining human personalities and life histories.

The existence of which of the following would tend to weaken the support for the hypothesis above most seriously?

A. A set of identical twins raised together who are shown by appropriate tests to have very similar value systems.

B. A pair of identical twins raised apart who differ markedly with respect to aggressiveness and other personality traits.

C. A younger brother and older sister raised together who have similar personalities and life experiences.

D. A mother and daughter who have the same profession even though they have very different temperaments.

E. A pair of twins raised together who have similar personality traits but different value systems.

4. People often do not make decisions by using the basic economic principle of rationally weighing all possibilities and then making the choice that can be expected to maximize benefits and minimize harm.

Routinely, people process information in ways that are irrational in this sense.

Any of the following, if true, would provide evidence in support of the assertions above EXCEPT:

A. People tend to act on new information, independent of its perceived relative merit, rather than on information they already have.

B. People prefer a major risk taken voluntarily to a minor one that has been forced on them, even if they know that the voluntarily taken risk is statistically more dangerous.

C. People tend to take up potentially damaging habits even though they have clear evidence that their own peers as well as experts disapprove of such behavior.

D. People avoid situations in which they could become involved in accidents involving large numbers of people more than they do situations where single-victim accidents are possible, even though they realize that an accident is more likely in the latter situations than in the former.

E. People usually give more weight to a physician's opinion about the best treatment for a disease than they do to the opinion of a neighbor if they realize that the neighbor is not an expert in disease treatment.

5. The Occupational Safety and Health Administration (OSHA) was established to protect workers from accidents and unsafe conditions on the job. There has actually been an increase in the number of job related accidents under OSHA. This demonstrates the agency's ineffectiveness.

Which of the following, if true concerning the period during which the increase occurred, most seriously weakens the argument above?

A. A number of job categories, excluded from the jurisdiction of OSHA in the legislation originally establishing the agency, have continued to be outside OSHA's jurisdiction.

B. OSHA has been assigned a greater number of kinds of workplace activities to monitor.

C. There has been an increase in the total number of people at work, and the ratio of work related deaths and injuries to size of work force has fallen in OSHA-supervised occupations.

D. Regulations issued by OSHA have met with political criticism from elected officials and the mass media.

E. The increase in job-related accidents has occurred mainly in a single job category, whereas the number of job-related accidents has remained approximately constant in other categories.

6. Companies are often torn between the benefits of focusing on one major product or service and the drawbacks of relying too heavily on one primary source of income. While narrow focus can provide a company with an advantage over competitors that offer a wider range of products or services, an undiversified income stream can leave a company susceptible to major fluctuations in cash flow. We can see this tension realized when, for example,_________________. Which of the following best completes the passage below?

A. a local messenger service known for its speedy deliveries is forced to lay off twenty percent of its work force after a rise in local taxes encourages many local businesses to move out of state

B. an advertising agency loses one of its clients

C. a holding company that owns a car rental agency and a national doughnut chain is now interested in purchasing a professional basketball team.

D. a construction company opts to use non-union labor to increase its profits.

E. a specialty sandwich store decides to open franchises throughout the country that will focus on using local ingredients

7. Calorie restriction, a diet high in nutrients but low in calories, is known to prolong the life of rats and mice by preventing heart disease, cancer,

diabetes, and other diseases. A six-month study of 48 moderately overweight people, who each reduced their calorie intake by at least 25 percent, demonstrated decreases in insulin levels and body temperature, with the greatest decrease observed in individuals with the greatest percentage change in their calorie intake. Low insulin level and body temperature are both considered signs of longevity, partly because an earlier study by other researchers found both traits in long-lived people.

If the above statements are true, they support which of the following inferences?

A. Calorie restriction produces similar results in humans as it does in rats and mice.

B. Humans who reduce their calorie intake by at least 25 percent on a long-term basis will live longer than they would have had they not done so.

C. Calorie intake is directly correlated to insulin level in moderately overweight individuals.

D. Individuals with low insulin levels are healthier than individuals with high insulin levels.

E. Some individuals in the study reduced their calorie intake by more than 25 percent.

Chapter 8

Answer Key

1. Solution – B

Conclusion

The larger farmers should adopt the same measures as the smaller farmers .They should use manures as fertilizers and save on operating costs. Then, they will be able to realise greater savings.

Assumption

The overall operating costs borne by many small farmers are reduced when the farmers eliminate expensive commercial chemical fertilizers and pesticides in favor of crop rotation and the twice-yearly use of manure as fertilizer.

A. It is more cost-effective for small farmers to eliminate the use of commercial fertilizers and pesticides than it is for large farmers to do so-

   This is a completely different issue that is not related to the main conclusion.

B. A sufficient amount of manure will be available for the fields of large farmers- This is the best possible answer, because somewhere the argument does assume that the amount of manure after

used by small farmers will still be available for large farmers which they will be able to use well and reduce the costs and gain better savings.

C. Large farmers would not realize similar cost benefits by using treated sewage sludge instead of commercial chemical fertilizers- This is a casual prediction which many not be true.

D. Large farmers generally look to small farmers for innovative ways of increasing crop yields or reducing operating costs- Again, an extreme conclusion based on unsupported evidence.

E. The smaller the farm, the more control the farmer has over operating costs- This may be true but there is no solid evidence to infer this.

2. Solution – C

Assumption

Some insects are able to feed on the leaves of milkweed, a toxic plant, by first cutting and draining the vein that secretes the toxin.

Conclusion

The method of detoxification guarantees that some insects will always be able to eat milkweed, because the plant could never evolve to produce a toxin that is lethal in the trace amounts left after the vein is cut.

A. The insects that successfully detoxify milkweed are not able to undergo the evolutionary changes necessary to allow them to detoxify other plants-

This is not the main point of the argument and therefore eliminated.

B. Unlike milkweed, other kinds of toxic plants would be able to overcome their vulnerabilities to predators through evolutionary changes- Again; overcoming vulnerabilities by other toxic plants is a deviation all together.

C. The toxin-carrying veins of the milkweed plant can never evolve in such a way that insects cannot cut through- This is the underlying assumption when the author concludes that the way insects cut the vein secreting the toxin, they will be able to eat the milkweed because the weed won't be able to evolve and produce the lethal toxin once the toxin vein is cut. Therefore, this is the right answer.

D. The method of detoxification used by insect predators of milkweed would not successfully detoxify other kinds of toxic plants- This is an extreme conclusion which is not based upon facts.

E. There are insects that use means other than draining the toxin in order to feed on toxic plants- Again a generalized prediction which might not be true.

3. Solution – B

Conclusion

Heredity is more important than environment in determining human personalities and life histories.

Premise

The conclusion was based on the study observation that identical twins who were raised apart in dissimilar environments found that in each case the twins were similar in character,medical history, and life experiences.

A. A set of identical twins raised together who are shown by appropriate tests to have very similar value systems – This stresses more on the role of heredity and environment in human behaviour and therefore eliminated.

B. A pair of identical twins raised apart who differ markedly with respect to aggressiveness and other personality traits.

   This is the most logical answer since it weakens the hypothesis that heredity is more important than environment. Here,it is clearly stated identical twins raised in different environments or apart differ markedly with respect to aggressiveness and other personality traits.

C. A younger brother and older sister raised together who have similar personalities and life experiences- This is a different context, not that of identical twins and therefore can have different results.

D. A mother and daughter who have the same profession even though they have very different temperaments. Again, a different sample compared to the original argument.

E. A pair of twins raised together who have similar personality traits but different value systems.

This strengthens the hypothesis that similar environment has similar personality traits but inconsistency with respect to the original argument and therefore eliminated.

4. Solution – E

Conclusion

People process information in ways that are irrational.

Assumption

People often do not make decisions by using the basic economic principle of rationally weighing all possibilities and then making the choice that can be expected to maximize benefits and minimize harm.

We have to basically choose an option that provides evidence to the fact that people don't always take irrational decisions and carefully weigh all the possibilities

A. People tend to act on new information, independent of its perceived relative merit, rather than on information they already have- This strengthens the conclusion and therefore not the answer.

B. People prefer a major risk taken voluntarily to a minor one that has been forced on them, even if they know that the voluntarily taken risk is statistically more dangerous- This also proves that people act irrationally and therefore eliminated.

C. People tend to take up potentially damaging habits even though they have clear evidence that their own peers as well as experts disapprove of such behavior- Again, evidence that people don't carefully weigh possibilities and fail to make rational decisions.

D. People avoid situations in which they could become involved in accidents involving large numbers of people more than they do situations where single victim accidents are possible, even though they realize that an accident is more likely in the latter situations than in the former- This also strengthens the main conclusion in the argument.

E. People usually give more weight to a physician's opinion about the best treatment for a disease than they do to the opinion of a neighbor if they realize that the neighbor is not an expert in disease treatment- This is the correct answer because it mentions about carefully weighing one possibility over the other and proves that people can say rational decisions.

5. Solution – C

Conclusion

There has actually been an increase in the number of job related accidents under OSHA. This demonstrates the agency's ineffectiveness.

Assumption

The Occupational Safety and Health Administration (OSHA) was established to protect workers from accidents and unsafe conditions on the job.

A. A number of job categories, excluded from the jurisdiction of OSHA in the legislation originally establishing the agency, have continued to be outside OSHA's jurisdiction- This is off the main point about increase in the number of accidents.

B. OSHA has been assigned a greater number of kinds of workplace activities to monitor- Again ,an allied point not focussing on the main conclusion.

C. There has been an increase in the total number of people at work, and the ratio of work related deaths and injuries to size of work force has fallen in OSHA-supervised occupations- This weakens the conclusion that OHSA has been ineffective in controlling accidents at work since the data contradicts the main conclusion and is thus the answer.

D. Regulations issued by OSHA have met with political criticism from elected officials and the mass media.

E. The increase in job-related accidents has occurred mainly in a single job category, whereas the number of job-related accidents has remained approximately constant in other categories.

6. Solution – A

Assumption

Companies are often torn between the benefits of focusing on one major product or service and the drawbacks of relying too heavily on one primary source of income.

Conclusion

While narrow focus can provide a company with an advantage over competitors that offer a wider range of products or services, an undiversified income stream can leave a company susceptible to major fluctuations in cash flow

Question

We can see this tension mentioned in the conclusion get realised with the following example:

A. a local messenger service known for its speedy deliveries is forced to lay off twenty percent of its work force after a rise in local taxes encourages many local businesses to move out of state-

This is an undiversified business which had to lay off twenty percent of its workforce after rise in taxes which made it susceptible to move out of state. This example is in line with the conclusion which focusses on fluctuations in cash flow and the disadvantages due to a single line of business or income and thus the answer.

B. an advertising agency loses one of its clients- This does not indicate why the agency lost clients and hence does not fit it in with the premise of the argument.

C. a holding company that owns a car rental agency and a national doughnut chain is now interested in purchasing a professional basketball team- This goes against the conclusion which talks about single income and here they talk about diversifying in basketball.

D. a construction company opts to use non-union labor to increase its profits- This is a deviation from the main point.

E. a specialty sandwich store decides to open franchises throughout the country that will focus on using local ingredients- Again a different point about local ingredients which might actually create more revenue than losses.

7. Solution – B

Fact

A six-month study of 48 moderately overweight people, who each reduced their calorie intake by at least 25 percent, demonstrated decreases in insulin levels and body temperature, with the greatest decrease observed in individuals with the greatest percentage change in their calorie intake.

Conclusion

Low insulin level and body temperature are both considered signs of longevity, partly because an earlier study by other researchers found both traits in long-lived people.

Assumption

Calorie restriction, a diet high in nutrients but low in calories, is known to prolong the life of rats and mice by preventing heart disease, cancer, diabetes, and other diseases.

Question

What is the inference if both statements are true. Based on the statements,it can be inferred that human calorie intake will increase longevity.

A. Calorie restriction produces similar results in humans as it does in rats and mice- This is not the main point in the argument.

B. Humans who reduce their calorie intake by at least 25 percent on a long-term basis will live longer than they would have had they not done so- This can be logically inferred from the data in the argument and therefore is the answer.

C. Calorie intake is directly correlated to insulin level in moderately overweight individuals- This is deviation from the main conclusion of whether calorie intake influences longevity.

D. Individuals with low insulin levels are healthier than individuals with high insulin levels- Again off the point ,talking about insulin levels and not calorie intake and longevity and illness.

E. Some individuals in the study reduced their calorie intake by more than 25 percent- Just a mere observation and not fulfilling the conclusion.

Author Bio

A dentist researcher by qualification but a mentor-writer by passion and profession, being an overseas education consultant and mentor, Dr. Jyuthica has wholeheartedly dedicated 15 years of her professional life to teaching English and verbal reasoning to students regionally, nationally and globally. She has constantly been striving for student benefit, contentment and development and has successfully placed hundreds of students abroad at prestigious universities. Her body of work can be determined as preparing students for GRE, GMAT, SAT and IELTS and guiding them comprehensively at every step of their overseas education. Her step into the writing world was through two academic books on exam preparations, and both of them have been received with a reassuring response.

The real her is about ruminating on the wonders of the universe, curiously researching abstract concepts such as the link between spirituality and the modern world, Indian Vedic culture and its application, body-soul relationship and communication and divine art.

Along with academic writing, creative writing especially on abstract topics and spheres such as mind, body, spirit, art, philosophy and thoughtful art has been her passion. Through her books, she wants to spread the message of purity, clarity, innocence and power of now. Writing in her opinion is a tête-à-tête with the world but through written words, thoughts and mute reflections. She believes that her writing is an eclectic mix of the various interests and career experiences she draws from and therefore is artsy yet scientific, abstract yet centred and humorous yet piercing.